Simple Bible Guide

Simple Bible Guide

Phil Sanders

ISBN - 978-0-6152-0668-4

Foreword

The author of this guide is not a pastor or doctor of theology, just a Christian called to write this document. I pray that you will find it useful.

All of us hunger for a relationship with the Lord, this desire is manifest in all humans. Have you felt unfulfilled, even though your life is pretty good? Is your life a mess with no hope for the future? These conditions and anything in between are indicators that God is reaching out to you.

The word of God tells us that we are all sinners and that God sent His only Son, Jesus Christ to earth to die for our sins. After he died on the cross for our sins he was resurrected and sent the Holy Spirit to us. The Bible is Gods' word and it says: Jesus said to him, "I am the way, the truth, and the life. No one comes to the Father except through Me" (John 14:6).

If you believe that Jesus Christ is your savior please pray for the Lord to open your heart and mind, and then pray:

Lord, I believe that I am a sinner and I accept you as my one and only Savior and trust only in you for my salvation. Lord would you send your spirit to change my life and bring me peace.

When you pray this prayer, and mean it with your whole being, you are saved and will have eternal life in heaven. Your sin is forgiven, and all your sins will be forgiven, for being saved does not mean we are not sinners. When you have accepted the Lord as your Savior the Bible will have new meaning to you.

Table of Contents

Introduction

This Bible guide is designed to be a simple way to introduce a person to the most important book in the world. The Bible is not only for Christians, but this guide is meant to provide a stepping stone to help new believers understand the basics of this awesome book.

A simple overview of the Bible is that the book has two main parts. The Old Testament is about the times before the Lord Jesus Christ came to earth to die for our sins and the New Testament is about after the Lord came to earth as the Son of God

You have probably heard before that Christians believe that the Bible is the Holy word of God. You may be curious about how the Bible was developed. Basically the Bible was developed using ancient manuscripts that were preserved, collected, and translated with Divine oversight to create the King James version and others translated in the same way.

No original documents were found, only copies of copies, but there is great evidence of their accuracy (see Isaiah for an example). The only way to explain how the Bible talks to people is that it is the Holy Word of God provided to us through divine inspiration so that we will know the truth.

A note about referencing the bible. When a verse is used it is described by the book or the abbreviation for the book and the chapter and verse; for example Matt 9:9, means the 9th chapter and 9th verse of the book of Matthew. Most Bibles have a number in front of each verse so that you can easily find the referenced material.

Bible study is the key to understanding God's word. As you get in the habit of regular study of the Bible you will be amazed at the things that speak to you.

In Chapter four there are resources for you to use to find more information about the Bible.

New Testament

Why start with the New Testament first? The New Testament is the account of Jesus Christ and the new covenant God made with all people through Jesus Christ. God speaks to believers through the whole bible, but the New Testament is especially helpful to new believers.

The first four books of the New Testament are called the Gospels. Gospel essentially means the word of God. These four books were written by disciples (a follower of Jesus Christ) two (Matthew and John) were members of the twelve apostles (a messenger) selected by the Lord to be with him during his time on earth.

Matthew

Matthew was a tax collector for the Romans. He was called by Jesus to be one of the 12 apostles in a very simple manner. As described in Matt 9:9 "As Jesus passed on from there, He saw a man named Matthew sitting at the tax office. And He said to him, "Follow Me." So he arose and followed Him". Matthews' gospel was written to his countrymen the nation of Israel, but is still relevant for all. He describes Jesus as the Messiah (the anointed

One from God, long awaited as His coming was prophesied many times in the Old Testament), the King of the Jews. A series of Old Testament quotations are used to show Jesus is the Messiah described in the Old Testament. Matthews' key message is that Jesus Christ is King. This is demonstrated through His genealogy, message and miracles.

Mark

Mark was the son of a woman named Mary (not the Mother of Jesus) whose home was a meeting place for the disciples. The key message of Marks' gospel is captured in this verse; "for even the Son of man came not to be ministered unto, but to minister, and to give his life a ransom for many" (10:45). Mark describes Jesus' as a servant, who taught, preached, and healed others even to his death.

Luke

Luke was a physician and he writes with compassion as he factually documents the perfect humanity of Jesus, the Son of Man. Luke moves precisely through Jesus' ancestry, early life, and then carefully and chronologically describes the Lord's early earthly ministry. He describes that the resurrection insures that "His purpose will be fulfilled; to seek and save that which was lost" (19:10).

John

The apostle John was one of Jesus closest friends during His ministry. John emphasizes the deity of Jesus, beginning the book with the pre-existence and describing the unity of God and Jesus. Johns' purpose throughout this powerful topical vice chronological gospel is crystal clear. The book revolves around seven miracles and seven "I am" statements of Jesus Christ. John's breathtaking eyewitness description of the upper room meal and the events leading to the resurrection provide dramatic proof that Jesus is the Son of God.

Acts

The book of Acts was written by Luke the physician. It is the story of the men and women who began to spread the news of a risen Savior to the most remote corners of the world. These people took the last words of Jesus as the great commission it was to them and indeed for all of us; "But you shall receive power when the Holy Spirit has come upon you; and you shall be witnesses to Me in Jerusalem, and in all Judea and Samaria, and to the end of the earth." (1:8). This work starts with the work of the Holy Spirit in the early believers and then describes works of Peter and early travels of Paul as they are sent out empowered by he Spirit.

Romans

The disciple Paul was chosen by God to lead the effort to bring the Gospel to the Gentile world. Romans' is arguably Paul's greatest work; placed first among his thirteen epistles (letters or messages) in the New Testament. This book records the most systematic presentation of the Christian doctrine in the Bible. The book powerfully brings the message that we are justified by faith, and describes practical theological exhortations for all believers.

1 Corinthians

The most important city in Greece during Paul's time was Corinth. This city was a key hub of world wide commerce and Paul founded a church here to spread the message. Paul's first letter addresses concerns and questions raised by believers in the church. He counsels them on problems and pressures of the church struggling in a pagan society. Paul addresses timeless problems such as immorality, questionable practices, abuses of the Lords' Supper, spiritual gifts, factions and lawsuits among believers.

2 Corinthians

Paul's second letter was written during his missionary journeys and is sent to the church at Corinth. False teachers had created concerns with the believers regarding the legitimacy of Paul as an apostle of Jesus. Paul's letter expresses his thanks to the majority of repentant people and to appeal to the minority still rebelling to accept his authority. This book describes and defends his legitimate calling as an apostle of Jesus Christ.

Galatians

Paul addresses the people at the churches he established in Galatia. He describes his credentials as an apostle with a message from God, separating himself from the Jewish teachers that had preached to the people after he left. He directly refuted the idea that circumcision was necessary to salvation and was not part of the gospel of Christ. Paul's letter to the Galatians is an attack against the gospel of works and defense of the gospel of faith and grace.

Ephesians

Paul wrote this letter during the time he was in prison in Rome. He speaks to a group of believers and describes the contents of the Christians' spiritual blessings; adoption, acceptance, wisdom, inheritance, the Holy Spirit, life, grace, redemption, forgiveness, and citizenship. This book is a great treatise for general use by Christians.

Philippians

This book provides instruction on Christian unity. The central though is simply that joy and unity are only possible in Christ. The purpose of this book was essentially a thank you to the believers at Philippi for the offering of financial support, to help with Paul's foreign missionary work. Although Paul supported himself working as a tentmaker, and rarely took money for preaching, this help from Philippe provided help in Paul's hour of need.

Colossians

Paul's purpose in this letter was to show that Christ is first and foremost in everything. Paul, in prison, had heard of a dangerous heresy that was occurring at the Church at Colosse. The heresy was resulting in a philosophy that called for the worship of angels as they were considered to be between God and man. Paul focuses on the deity of Christ and the direct relationship with man and addresses the issue both doctrinally and practically in the book.

1 Thessalonians

Paul opens this book reminding the believers of good memories of the time he spent in Thessalonica and presents a stirring argument for vindication of his conduct that directly contradicts what the false teachers were saying about him.

This letter mentions the coming of the Lord in every chapter, and closes with a powerful instruction regarding the return of the Lord as the hope and comfort for believers.

2 Thessalonians

In this book Paul's primary issue is addressing a misunder-standing regarding the coming day of the Lord. False teachers had spread reports that the day of the Lord had already come, this false doctrine caused some believers to waiver in their faith. Paul presents the powerful case for a future day after the great falling away, or apostasy, as the time for the second coming of Christ.

1 Timothy

Paul sent letters to Timothy and Titus that are often called the pastoral letters. These epistles have been used as guidance by pastors, and indeed all Christians, on key aspects of church behav-ior for centuries. Paul lays out the task of pastors, these tasks have always been challenging, even as they are today. He lays out three primary tasks; false doctrine must be erased, public worship safe-guarded, and mature leadership developed

2 Timothy

Paul's second letter to Timothy is written from prison, where he is expecting execution. He assures Timothy of his continuing love and prayers, and reminds him of his spiritual heritage. Paul warns of the coming efforts of mankind to corrupt the Gospel. As the Gospel is attacked men will desert the truth. Paul power-fully describes his future with the Lord and how his life was used to serve Christ.

Titus

Paul writes this letter to Titus concerning the Churches of Crete. Titus, a young pastor is faced with the assignment of bring-ing order to the Church at Crete. Paul advises him to appoint men of proven spiritual character to oversee the work of the church. This letter has an emphasis on the proper view of good works. Paul makes it crystal clear that we are saved by God's mercy and not by works, but we have obligations in faith.

Philemon

Paul wrote this letter to the Colossians while in prison. This letter is sent to a brother in the Lord, Philemon. Paul writes to Philemon on behalf of Onesimus a runaway former Roman slave owned by Philemon. Onesimus is now a brother in Christ and Paul appeals to Philemon to receive him back as he would Paul himself.

Paul shows how brotherly Christian love really works in tough situations.

Hebrews

This letter to Jewish Christians has many Old Testament quotes to support the statements it makes. An important message is in 4:12-13 "For the word of God is living and active. Sharper than any double-edged sword, it penetrates even to dividing soul and spirit, joints and marrow; it judges the thoughts and attitudes of the heart. Nothing in all creation is hidden from God's sight. Everything is uncovered and laid bare before the eyes of him to whom we must give account." This is a powerful appeal to live he Christian life apart from ritual and tradition.

James

The book of James is from Jesus' brother to Jewish believers. He stresses that true faith manifests itself through works of faith. He synthesizes true faith and practical experience covering vital topics; perseverance, trials, wisdom, faith, the tongue, and explaining their impact on true faith. The information he provides on the power of the tongue is critical for believers.

1 Peter

Peter, the leader of the Lords' 12 disciples writes this letter to the churches in Asia minor, modern day Turkey. He writes to believers struggling with persecution and admonishes all believers that they will be attacked by the enemy. Peter encourages all to be courageous when attacked for Christ. He calls for submission, wives to husbands, of husbands to wives, of citizens to government, and Christians to each other.

2 Peter

In first Peter problems from the outside are dealt with, in the second book Peter deals with problems within the Church. Peter warns of false teachers that will rise up and preach false doctrines. He appears to address both the present times and the future and warns that before the second coming of the Lord there would a falling away. This apostasy would be of an appalling magnitude led by ungodly men and hypocrites who would fill the church with doctrines of evil.

1 John

John shares about Love throughout this book. He also addresses assurance of eternal life. He describes how we know that we who have believed in Jesus as our Savior have eternal life. John knew that new believers would have salvation, but that they would need to grow into assurance of that salvation. He warns of two key roadblocks for Christians. First is falling in love with worldly things and second falling for the lies of false teachings.

2 John

John wrote this letter to a chosen lady, that could have been a person or a church as the church is considered the bride of Jesus. He tells about the truth in the Lord and to caution readers about false teachers.

3 John

John's third letter encourages Christian brothers to have fellowship with one another. He emphasizes truth and prays for a church leader's (Gaius) persistent walk in the truth.

Jude

This book is widely held to have been written by Jesus' brother Judas (in some forms Jude). Jude starts the letter focusing on followers common salvation and then sternly warns about false teachers. He builds a strong foundation for all to fight for the faith against the false teachers. He encourages believers to be spiritually prepared to answer the summons to defend the faith.

Revelation

John also wrote Revelation, the only New Testament book focusing primarily on prophetic events. The book of Revelation is also known as the Apocalypse. Both the Latin Revelation and the Greek Apocalypse mean the same thing; an uncovering. Revelation describes the age to come when the name of God is vindicated before all creation. This final book of the Bible is centered on the second coming of Jesus Christ, who has authority to judge the earth, re-make it and rule it forever and ever.

Genesis

Genesis is the first book of the Bible, known as he book of beginnings. God wants us to know that he created everything. This part of the Bible describes our Lord's creation and the garden of Eden.

The garden of Eden is where God put the first people that He created. He made man and named him Adam, then He made woman (Eve). Adam and Eve were with God in Eden. The garden of Eden also had a snake called the serpent (satan). God told Adam and Eve not to eat the fruit of a special tree. The serpent lied to Eve and told her that it would be good to eat fruit from the tree, that it would make her like God. First Eve ate the fruit and then Adam ate some too. God punished Adam and Eve for their disobedience by sending them from the garden of Eden because they had become sinners with a fallen nature and thus were separated from God. He also said they and all of their decedents would have to work and suffer, compared to living in the garden of Eden with God. He said that people would have control over all the other animals he made. After he flooded the earth He made a covenant with his people that we still see as true today. In chapter 9, verse 13 it says: "I do set my bow in the cloud, and it shall be for a token of a covenant between me and the earth."

Throughout the Bible God shows his love for all of us. Even though he banished Adam and Eve from Eden he still loved all people, he demonstrated this by giving hope that some day people who believe on His Son Jesus can have eternal life with Him.

Exodus

This second Old Testament book is about the oppression of the Hebrew people by the Egyptians, their deliverance by God, and then describes the departure of these people from Egypt. This book describes important theological foundations that remain relevant today. The Ten Commandments are first introduced in this book and God lays out critical information about Himself, His name, redemption, law, and how He is to be worshipped. The foundation of all organizations comes from the Lords instructions to Moses on how to organize the people.

Leviticus

The third book of the Bible is essentially a rule book. The book's name indicates that it primarily relates to the duties of the Levites. The Levites were the tribe designated by God to be priests. This book of laws was given to Israel by God through Moses at Mount Sinai. This book also provides a critical key to the most important event (at least to all that are born again) of all time, the death of Jesus to atone for all of our sins. While some may think that the laws given to the Israelites traveling in the middle-eastern desert are not important today they may be surprised by the current relevancy. Some of our dietary and medical practices today continue to implement these laws, of course using improved technology.

Numbers

This book describes the journey of the people of Israel (estimated to be several hundred thousand up to two million people) to the promised land, guided by God's divine providence. The Journey took 40 years and only three men who were alive (over twenty years old) at the beginning survived to the end, and only two of them made it into the promised land. The people disobeyed the

Lord and were punished which is why only two of the original number make it into the promised land.

Numbers 32:13, The Lords anger burned against Israel and he made them wander in the desert forty years, until the whole generation of those who had done evil in his sight was gone.

A key message for all is that through the turmoil God is trustworthy and delivers on the covenant he made with this people to get them to the promised land.

Deuteronomy

This book is a repetition of the laws recorded in Exodus, Leviticus, and Numbers. These laws were put in one book for the people who were to settle in the promised land. This book is more than just laws, it spells out a treaty between God and his chosen people.

A very important theological concept is found in Deuteronomy chapter 6 verse 5: "Love the LORD your God with all your heart and with all your soul and with all your strength".

Joshua

This book tells of God's people entering the promised land after wandering in the desert for forty years. God's people have much warfare with the peoples that already populate the land. These peoples have many evil beliefs and practices. God fights and wins battles with the evil peoples and gives Joshua strength to lead the people. Joshua's faith in God is demonstrated throughout this book, in 24:15 he says; "And if it seems evil to you to serve the LORD, choose for yourselves this day whom you will serve, whether the gods which your fathers served that were on the other side of the River, or the gods of the Amorites, in whose land you dwell. But as for me and my house, we will serve the Lord."

Judges

After the death of Joshua the Hebrew nation was a confederacy of 12 independent tribes. Judges describes approximately 300 years of oppression and deliverance. The book tells the history of seven cycles of sin to salvation showing how the nation of Israel sets aside God's law and substituted what they wanted. During this period God raises up seven rulers, as part of each of the seven cycles, called Judges to restore the nation to God's law.

Ruth

The main themes of this book are; love, devotion, and redemption. This story is set in the dark days of the judges. Ruth was a Moabite woman who forsakes her pagan heritage and clings to the God of Israel. Because of her faithfulness in God rewards her by giving her a new husband (Boaz) a son and a privileged position in the lineage of David and Christ (she is the grandmother of David).

First Samuel

Samuel was a judge and this book describes the transition of leadership in Israel from judges to kings. The book features three characters. Samuel, the last judge and prophet; Saul, the first king of Israel; and David, the king-elect. Samuel anointed as king both Saul and David moving the nation from the period of judges to kings. .

Second Samuel

Second Samuel focuses on the highlights of the reign of king David. The story describes his ascension to the throne and his reign first over Judah, and the over the whole nation of Israel. David's sins of adultery and murder and the consequence of those sins on his family and the entire nation are detailed. This book also tells of God's promise of an everlasting kingdom, important information for all believers.

First Kings

This book has two primary themes, in the first half the focus is the life of Solomon and Israel's rise to the peak of size and glory. The story includes some of Solomon's great accomplishments including the splendor of the temple in Jerusalem. The second half of this book describes the history of two sets of kings and nations. These nations' peoples are disobedient and grow indifferent to God's instructions.

Second Kings

Second Kings continues the story of the two nations from First Kings. This book describes the monarchs of Israel and Judah. In Israel evil kings, nineteen consecutively, rule leading to captivity of the nation by Assyria. In Judah Godly kings sometimes ruled to reform some of the nations' evils and they continued for 130 years after the fall of Israel. Judah was conquered the people taken captive by the Babylonians and Jerusalem was destroyed.

First Chronicles

The books of First and Second Chronicles cover the same period of history as Second Samuel through Second Kings. Second Samuel through Second Kings looks at the period through a political historical context. Chronicles describes the era from a religious historical context.

Second Chronicles

Second Chronicles parallels First and Second Kings, but does not discuss the northern kingdom (Israel). This book only discusses the southern kingdom (Judah) because Israel refused to acknowledge the temple in Jerusalem. Chronicles generally focuses on kings that patterned their behavior after King David.

Ezra

Ezra a priest, traditionally known as the author of Chronicles and this book, continues the narrative of Second Chronicles. He describes how God fulfills His promise by returning His people to the promised land after seventy years in exile. The nations' second journey, this time from Babylon, includes a small fraction of the people because only a remnant of them chose to leave Babylon.

Nehemiah

The book of Nehemiah, cupbearer to the King in the Persian palace, is about the third and last return to Jerusalem after the exile to Babylon. Nehemiah leads the rebuilding of the wall of Jerusalem. After several years of delays the task is completed in only 52 days. This remarkable achievement shows the people that this could only be done with God's enabling.

Esther

Esther was a beautiful Jewish girl that was selected to be queen replacing a disobedient queen who was an evil woman. The story in this book demonstrates God's protection of His people. Significant events occur that made possible great future events. These events include Haman's plot to bring grave danger to the Jews which is countered by Esther's courage.

Job

Job is set in the time of the patriarchs (Abraham, Isaac, Jacob, and Joseph). The book of Job tells the story of a man who was rich in every way who Satan accuses to God of being faithful only because of his blessings. After receiving permission from God, Satan tortures Job in an attempt to get him to curse God. Job suffers greatly but does not curse God and loses everything his wealth, family, and health. Indeed after his property is taken and his children killed he is made sick with boils covering his body creating incredible suffering. In the end Job maintains his faith in God and receives back more than he had before his trials.

Psalms

Psalms were essentially songs in the age they were written, this book contains over 150 songs. Virtually every psalm praises God. The psalms are about the human experience from the creation through the ages up to when they were written by King David.

Proverbs

The book of Proverbs describes God's detailed instructions for dealing with the practical aspects of life. Solomon is held to be the principal author of this book. He uses a combination of poetry, parables, and short stories that deliver a divine perspective for dealing with life's issues.

Ecclesiastes

This book, also traditionally believed to be principally written by Solomon, shows how nothing can fill the void in man's life except God. Solomon was the wisest, richest, most influential person in kingdom and he describes the futile emptiness of being apart from God as "vanity". Vanity is indeed the key word in this book.

The Song of Solomon

This book is a love song written by Solomon. It has been interpreted many ways. Some Jewish interpretations indicate it is a story of the exodus. Christians have interpreted the story to be about Christ and His church. Others believe it is simply a love song heralding the virtues of married love.

Isaiah

Isaiah is called the messianic prophet because he was convinced and prophesied so much and so accurately that God would send man the Messiah. Interestingly Isaiah has sixty six chapters, just like the Bible. The last 27 chapters focus on the coming of the Messiah as Savior. Isaiah made 19 specific prophecies about the

Messiah, approximately 750 years before Jesus came, that have proven incredibly accurate. Our Bible accuracy was amazingly confirmed when a 2000 year old text of the book of Isaiah was discovered with the dead sea scrolls in the 1940's and it was virtually identical to the Bible text.

Jeremiah

Jeremiah, for more than 40 years, prophecies a message of doom to the people of Israel. He steadfastly preached that the apostasy of the people would result in destruction. He faithfully told them that surrender to God's will was the only way for the people to be rescued from disaster. The people continued to worship idols and not obey God's instructions. This resulted in destruction of the southern kingdom of Judah by the Babylonians as Jeremiah had predicted.

Lamentations

Jeremiah tells the story of the once proud Jerusalem that was destroyed by the Babylonians. He uses five poems to tell the sad story. He continues his compelling message about the faithfulness of God. He finds for himself, and others that would listen, hope in his faith in God's perfect will.

Ezekiel

The book of Ezekiel is about a priest and prophet ministering during the seventy year Babylonian captivity. This story is about the bleakest days in Judah's history. Ezekiel faithfully preaches the message of God to His people in captivity. God's message is reassurance that the exiled people will be reassembled and made a nation again. Powerful prophecy about the future, some that are coming true in our times, for example, Israel is back in it's land after 1900 years without a home.

Daniel

Daniel was the primary author and principal character in this book. Daniel's name means "God is my judge" and his ministry spanned the seventy year Babylonian captivity. He was a prophet of God and proclaimed God's eternal purpose. Daniel preaches about his dreams that were inspired by God. Daniel documents powerful miracles and prophecies about the future. Incredibly accurate and powerful prophecies include the coming of Jesus as the Messiah and about the end times correlating with the book of Revelations.

Hosea

Hosea ministers in the northern kingdom, Israel. The nation is enjoying a time of prosperity. But, sins of moral corruption and spiritual adultery are rampant among the people. Hosea is commanded by God to marry Gomer, an adulterous wife. Their marriage is interrupted as a dramatization of the unfaithfulness of God's people. Hosea preaches a three prong message; God hates His peoples' sins, His judgment is certain, and God's love is undying.

Joel

Joel's theme is God's sovereign work in history showing that the courses of man and nature are according to His will. When locusts blanket the land and strip it of living green thing in a matter of hours Joel seizes the event to proclaim God's message. The book predicts the Gospel age and the coming of the Holy Spirit and the coming judgment as described in Revelations.

Amos

Amos was a farmer turned prophet. He prophesied during a period when the rich claimed to be religious, but made their splendor on the backs of the poor. God had already disciplined the nation twice and forgiven twice, Amos preached the nearness of God's judgment, which came about when the Assyrians captured them and put them in captivity.

Obadiah

Obadiah predicts the total destruction of the Edomites who had participated over time with several enemy attacks on Jerusalem. He describes their crimes as the basis for their judgment and that they will be as if they never were. With the destruction of Jerusalem in A.D. 70 this prophecy was completed.

Jonah

Jonah rejects God's call to preach the announcement of the coming judgment to Nineveh, the capital of Assyria, mortal enemies of his own country. God then causes him to be in the belly of a big fish for 3 days and nights to convince Jonah that He is serious. Jonah preaches to the wicked Ninevites. When the Ninevites repent and are forgiven by God. Jonah is angry and discouraged. God shows him through a vine about God's compassion for sinful men, even the enemies of His people.

Micah

Micah called to be a prophet foretells of the birth of the Messiah in Bethlehem. This book is roughly divided into thirds with different messages in each third. One third shows the sins of the nations. Another third describes the coming punishment of God. The final third promises hope for restoration after the discipline. There is a clear theme about God's righteous demands to walk with God.

Nahum

After Nineveh had heard Jonah, repented, and been forgiven of sins by God, the Ninevites had forgotten Him and returned to their old ways. Nahum declares that Nineveh will have a great downfall. He describes the destruction of the city as punishment from God for unrepentant sins. The city is utterly destroyed, with no trace, which fulfills prophecy.

Habakkuk

The lesson of this book is that the righteous will live by faith, even if the fulfillment of God's promise is a long way off. Habakkuk asks God specific questions and receives answers about why the wicked seem to prosper and the righteous seem suffer. He does not completely understand the answers, but they convince him of God's wisdom and faithfulness to His promises.

Zephaniah

This book shows that Zephaniah preached with a forceful prophesy about the judgment day coming. He clearly foretold of the destruction of Judah and other nations by the Babylonians, which came about shortly after the prophecy. The day of the Lord judgment prophesies can also be linked to the book of Revelations speaking about the second coming of the Lord.

Haggai

Haggai preached after the Babylonian exile. He preached fiery sermons to the people exhorting them to rebuild the temple of Jerusalem. The work of rebuilding had been stalled for over 15 years. Haggai's inspired words had immediate effects, the temple rebuilding started within a matter of months.

Zechariah

While Zechariah, along with Haggai also encouraged to the people to rebuild the temple of Jerusalem he also preached messianic prophecy. Nine specific prophecies about Jesus Christ, including one specifically concerning His death, would come true.

Malachi

The book of Malachi is the final book of the Old Testament, to the people of God. The nation, after being freed from Babylonian captivity was once again sinful. Malachi's message of coming judgment is both for the people of his time and for all of us as it relates to the end times with the second coming of the Lord.

Resources

The internet is a great source of Bible and spiritual knowledge. Here are a few places that will help in your walk with the Lord.

All About God - www.allaboutGod.com –

This website has excellent information with answers to many questions about God.

Blue Letter Bible – www.blueletterbible.org –

This website has outstanding information about the Bible, has great study tools.

Calvary Chapel – www.calvarychapel.com – Calvary Chapel is a non-denominational Christian church. Calvary has established affiliate Calvary Chapels across the world and is among the world's largest churches. It is one of the ten largest Protestant churches in the United States.

Salvation

If you believe that Jesus Christ is your savior please pray for the Lord to open your heart and mind, and then pray:

Lord, I believe that I am a sinner and I accept you as my one and only Savior and trust only in you for my salvation. Lord would you send your spirit to change my life and bring me peace.

When you pray this prayer, and mean it with your whole being, you are saved and will have eternal life in heaven. Your sin is forgiven, and all your sins will be forgiven, for being saved does not mean we are not sinners. When you have accepted the Lord as your Savior the Bible will have new meaning to you.

About Skybow Group

Skybow Group is a communications organization. We are founded in Christian principles, the name comes from the King James Version of the Bible, Genesis 9:13 - I do set my bow in the cloud, and it shall be for a token of a covenant between me and the earth.